KwaNobuhle Overcast

KwaNobuhle Overcast

Ayanda Billie

ISBN 978-0-9947104-3-7
ebook ISBN: 978-1-928476-29-0

Deep South
contact@deepsouth.co.za
www.deepsouth.co.za

Distributed in South Africa by
University of KwaZulu-Natal Press
www.ukznpress.co.za

Distributed worldwide by
African Books Collective
PO Box 721, Oxford, OX1 9EN, UK
www.africanbookscollective.com/publishers/deep-south

Deep South and the author acknowledge the financial assistance
of the National Arts Council for the production of this book

NATIONAL ARTS COUNCIL
OF SOUTH AFRICA

and a financial contribution from VW Community Trust

Earlier versions of some of these poems were published in
Tyhini 2014, Tyhini 2015, Illuminations 32 (Summer 2017) and
the jazz poetry anthology *To Breathe into Another Voice* (2017)

Cover design: Liz Gowans and Robert Berold
Text design and layout: Liz Gowans
Cover painting: Bretten-Anne Moolman, *Human Gestures No 92*

Contents

I

If I want to breathe   10

Primus stove   11

Sunday morning   12

I saw all this   13

Birth mark   14

Survival   15

I am not the only one   16

The empty house   17

There is no dog   18

When they hijacked me   19

If I could tell you   20

Dying moon   21

I'm forgetting how to live   22

Bones   23

KwaNobuhle overcast   24

II

All your tears   26

Still waiting   27

All they know   28

Thabo   29

She waits   30

Buyile   31

Letter from prison   32

Screams at the carwash   33

Blue collar   35

On a hospital bed   36

A life in pieces   37
Man cannot live like this   38

III

In the midst of all this   40
Morning star dance   41
A stone   42
No time for amagwijo   43
I cannot distance myself   44
Apartheid   45
I want to hide   46
From a distance   47
Time and words   48
Before the night ends   49
Qamata   50
Mankunku called the stars   51
Horn screaming   52
The trumpet note   53
In the morning   54
On this day   55
Finding love   56
I love you   57
Poem for you   58
Written in silence   59
Beginning of a song   60

In memory of Mziwoxolo Palie Sidzumo

If I want to breathe

i've learnt to love what I see
it has been like this
since I first saw the sun

i have to sleep at night
especially on weekends
beyond the cries
and inyakanyaka music
from my neighbours
who sometimes rejoice at nothing

sometimes i have to let go
of things i should have stood against

i don't want to be forgotten by history
only to be remembered
by the streets of kwa-nobuhle

in the dark and shining hours
if i still want to breathe
let me love this moment
                    and myself in it.

Primus stove

Even today
each time i enter the kitchen
of my grandmother
i am struck by the smell of paraffin
that still floats through those walls

Even today
each time i see the primus stove in the window
of dajees shop at durban street
i am fixed to its glare
as if it's saying something

Even today
each time i see old man cirha
on his rusty wheelchair
i am still taken by the gift of his hands
that once repaired our primus stove
then we had supper
and we licked our plates.

Sunday morning

Sunday morning after 10 am
he closed a rusty gate
wearing a black and white suit
with a bible in his left hand
a zol in his mouth
a chest full of the pain
of generations
and his grandson running behind him.

I saw all this

In daylight
bitterly cold
        you came running
        to force a woman
        with a child on her back
        out of her house

In daylight
everything trembled
        you came in full force
        with red-ants
to tear shacks apart
        suddenly it rained.

Birth mark

This township is unforgiving
It breaks up homes
Drives boys to smoke tik
Nyaope and all colourful substances
To dance on the ceiling naked
Laugh at their mothers crying

Boys become hyenas at night
Find their dreams in dustbins
Klap their fathers
Their skins taste of salt behind prison cells
Show no trace of their birth.

Survival

With the shapes of black survival
Sun, you fill
The growing chaos of the day
Sickle-clouds --
With the gentle embraces
Of a newborn,
And with presence of ancestors
Abaphantsi iminyanya
All around the contested terrain
The sun shines with such red light
Upon the township
Where the bornfree generation
Live, decay and die –
A dark future hangs
Over the grant grandchild
Shadows swallowed
By the funeral processions
Every Saturday morning

I am not the only one

The sky is blue
But we accept its greyness
I am not the only one
Who thinks that they lied to us
Heaven is not for the poor

On my way to the spaza shop
They are assembled
Like bats in a cave

A group of boys without moustaches
With okapis on their back pockets
Ready to stir the peace
Sorry Buda ndicela R2

They can make you dance
Without music playing
You will leave this earth
Without saying goodbye
To your children.

The empty house

School children walk in the black streets; the gravel road
      rustles quietly
Through the noise of the taxis screaming –
      town, town, town
In the grey alleys
A pack of dogs moves in ranks
From street to street
Following a hot bitch around dark corners
In the collapsing rdp houses
Decay looks out through broken windows;
A tired grandmother sits on a three-legged couch
      breathing heavily in the wind.
Morning in the empty house, a longing for the laughter
      of children.

There is no dog

my neighbour's dog is dead
swollen & skew
with tyre prints on its chest

the sun is melting its flesh
it's starting to rot
the smell travels
crossing the rubbish dump and shacks

now the day is beginning to rust
there is no dog next door
to howl to the moon

or bark at monsters nezithunzela
when they enter my yard
in darkness

still
the cars don't stop
for anything

When they hijacked me

i gave them the keys
i did not protest
because i was asking God
why in front of my child

If I could tell you

If I could tell you
About my life in fragments
Dig what I have forgotten
From under the earth
It would console an angry sea

My best poem
Is my life and tears
I hope it won't leave a stain
Of a dying heart in you
A curse to a dancing sun

Dying moon

The moon
starts to crack
we listen to its call
The howl
keeps rising
in darkness

We look through the window
dog at the gate
owl on the pole
staring at the crescent moon
warning us with eyes
that see through human bones

It's a bad omen for us
when we hear
its familiar cry
a sorrow song
tikoloshe will come
into our house
we stay indoors
and call the children inside

I'm forgetting how to live

let me say it again
i have realised
i'm forgetting how to live
my lips are dry
from not talking to others
recently, i'm annoyed by the sun

the township throws the baggage of its street
on my shoulders to carry
so that others may find their balance
jesus left a long a time ago
he said he would return
to take us away
until this day i'm still counting the stars

so let me say it again
these streets refuse to sleep
they always have gory stories
to tell in the morning
i drag the sky to weep with me
since i'm afraid
of carrying the basket of tears alone

Bones

brutality is bare in our township
staring at our god
pleading with the voice of a child
who is full of scars

marvin gaye once asked
"what's going on"
as if he knew his fate

the news soaks my heart in vinegar
what is left for now
are people eating other people
sitting at a dinner table
with their children peacefully

and the bones rattling
on a plate

KwaNobuhle overcast

I walk alone
in your bare streets without trees
adapt to every season
change my mood if it's overcast
like a chameleon on a branch

KwaNobuhle just for once
keep those who can make you
a place to raise children
not this sulphurous cage
where we watch dreams suffocate

Everything is dying here
you were once the colourful stars
until the floodgates opened
the Somalis took
all the shops in your streets

The Chinese squashed
your children into a corner
now it's they who
put the bread and salt
in your kitchen

You are no longer the same
you are like one who is afraid of the sea
to deny himself the fish
to feed his children

KwaNobuhle I wake up
to live like a limping bird
and smile at the four walls
of an RDP house.

All your tears

the kitchen is deserted
and the house is nothing
just a vanished song
a broken broom in the corner
an old smell of lavender polish
from the tile floor

in the yard a man without an ID
a man soaked by all your tears
a man from your semen
who cleans houses around the township
drags dead dogs and donkeys
that the municipality leaves to rot
to a dumping site

he is no man to anyone except to you
he is your child
just for once speak to him
speak to him even in his sleep
invade his dreams
tell him
the world belongs to him also

Still waiting

on
a pavement
in this township

i watched you
scratching
your chiskop

i heard the sound
of your teeth
turning to sand

we were young then
longed for the sun
to light the future

now
i hear you are working
as a petrol attendant
in king williams town

still waiting
for your life to
begin.

All they know

after Han-Shan

When men see uQhingqa
they run away
they say he is possessed
by amafufunyana

Always dressed in rags
with acrid smell of human flesh
dragging black plastic bags
through the streets wandering

No one understands
what he always mumbles
all he says to those he meets:
"kuyatsha kuyatsha, cima"

Thabo

stutters when he speaks
always asks for two rands
for cigarettes

a neighbour found him
naked drunk
on top of his grandmother

he cried
and cried
said he'd been bewitched

She waits

she paces up and down at the factory gate
sweating like a fighting bull
with one broken-heel shoe in her hand

she is waiting
to rip out the heart of the father
of the child trapped on her back
crying helplessly

he clocks out in a rush
in his blue overall
carrying a lunchbox
and a daily sun paper in one hand

"buti he's your child also
what do you think he will eat?"
the man forces a cold smile
trying to calm the beast
he digs into his wallet
and takes out mandela notes
without an utterance
looking deep
into her accusing eyes

she grabs them
stashes them in her breast
leaves him frozen
his head spinning

he stands there
listening to the footsteps
of other workers
rushing to their own miseries

Buyile

he was that breed that was touched
by the humbleness of sobukwe
so they came for him
ama-comrade necklaced him
in broad daylight
while children were watching

after seven days
ama-afrika buried him
when the sun stood still

when they filled the grave
with the last scoop of the soil
anger evaporated
the police were there at a distance
watching with a smile
when open palms were raised
 – izwe lethu i-africa!

later ama-comrade came again
to dig him out from his grave
in the presence of the police
they burnt him in his coffin
screaming "mayibuye i-afrika!"

Letter from prison

for Mzwandile Matiwane

Behind these four pages
I see your bearded face
in a letter I found
in a hanging letterbox
with the red stamp
of correctional services

I see the guards
in their deep brown uniforms
keys swinging on their waists
shouting your name
at visiting hour

I hear the noise
of the gates opening
the guard leading you
to the visiting room
after searching you
from head to toe
and the doors closing
behind you

Screams at the carwash

I

you drank
a bottle of commando brandy
only the two of you
while washing cars, staggering
drunk, humming a gospel song
and calling women passing by
amagqwirha and amahule

later you complained of a violent stomach
before you fell on your face
into the mud and lay quietly
they called you
your tongue hanging out
vomiting blood
you died that saturday
your body tired of the torture

II

numbers have dropped here
this carwash is not the same without you
the rain won't stop
is it you crying
or the gods
on seeing your bruises

rasta, your absence has left a hole
your shoes are too big to fit
others refuse your death
hoping to see you the next day
only to find
your orange bucket of water empty

III

my eyes used to follow you
when cleaning my car
i never trusted you
sometimes i would be unkind to you

i still have your image hiding
i have not forgotten how you looked
your dirty sagging trousers
a rotten smell from your nike takkies

Blue collar

on a factory floor
dreams expire

no comfort in routine
life is defined
by 8 hours

of clocking
in and out
of here

days and weeks
in tight
safety shoes

the same scream
from the bell
on top of us

disrupts
our ten minutes
of tea time

On a hospital bed

mkhuluwa
we held up
the somali shopkeeper

with okapis
in daylight
with children inside

i looked him dead
in the eyes

we want money
wena

with a pleading voice he said
why my friend?

i gave him one hole
in the chest

who's your friend
kwerekwere

i got mad
he fell
i rushed to the till

now i find myself here
in chains

not even a single visit
from my friends.

A life in pieces

Under the bridge
Zinc house stares
At the dump hive,
Man caged by a need
Of bread
Cat sitting at the stove,
Yelling at his shadow
Anger pushes through his chest,
On a Sunday morning
He grabs an empty
Paint tin
Belt around his neck
Kicks the tin
Chokes, eyes wide open
Swinging, grabbing
Breath jumps out
Dirty life ended
No one spoke of him.

Man cannot live like this

It was dark when he woke up
found himself all alone soaked in urine
appetite and all his senses lost
afraid of the dark
like a man who once saw
what was not meant to be seen

In the morning
sun glowing
he went out into the streets
to find the woman
at the taxi rank
selling vegetables
wearing a rainbow face
and a forgiving heart

It started to rain,
scent of wet soil
fresh like love
they both cried
birds flew away to their nest
with wet feathers.

In the midst of all this

I have indigestion of the soul
I drift into vague sleep
In the empty air that surrounds us

I am a widowed house
I find things because
I wander

I return
To what I am
Or what I dream I am

In the abandoned regions of the streets
I hear time falling
Drop by drop

I've made a hollow
I can abandon myself to life
In a dark room dreaming.

Morning star dance

after federico garcia lorca

in silence
>>> you dance
>> barefooted

>> wordless
>> in melodies
>> of warbling birds

dancing
>>> in motions

>> of an upright bass

>>> morning star hovers
>> above our dark pit

dancing
>> to empty
>> mystic yearnings
>> and begin once more
>> to live.

A stone

people say
rather trust a stone
than a human
a stone will not
break your heart
a stone will not complain
after a long day of work

i wish my poems
could be like stones
if thrown into the green sea
they will stay there
until the next generation
dives to the deep
to look for them.

No time for amagwijo

president
i have no time for a song
      for dolo phezulu
      for viva chief yam
      wathint'abafazi wathint' imbokodo

i have no time for toyi-toyi
i have come to give you a message
from the streets blocked with burning tyres
from the empty jojo tanks in the villages
from the children whose schools are locked for months

i have come to force you to look at my face
its tears running towards a dry river

i have come to show you
      rage, bitterness
      hopelessness and disillusion
stone-throwing at passing cars
i have not come here to count the stars
and make sketches in the sand
babies are dying at dora nginza hospital

I cannot distance myself

I have no ownership of land nor sky
I have become accustomed
To the country of myself
Whenever I open up myself
I'm left with wounds bleeding
From the swellings of the past
Gasps from the winter sun

Marikana martyrs died
From bullets bought with my taxes
All that matters to me is at risk
Whether i do something or nothing
They will always come back to me
I cannot distance myself from anything
There are cracks everywhere
Growling intestines

Still, i am standing in my country
I have something to do to offer
Working in a factory or anywhere
Man's work is never completed
It ends when a star disappears
From sight forever
A new date is recorded
And the body is washed away

Apartheid

Do not talk about apartheid
Forget about it
The smell of teargas, kicking of doors
Naked black bodies in mortuaries
Sink the past with bloodstain
In a dishwashing basin
We must not lose ourselves over nothing
Let us hug the beast
And carry the hopes of wounded hearts
Baptize our children
In the name of a cruel religion

I want to hide

i feel pain from the sky to the earth
let me go, i'm wounded
let me roll a zol with nesta marley
the dreaded philosopher
go looking for three little birds
to sing for me

From a distance

like a wailing
like a waterfall
                    like wind hitting
                    corrugated walls
                    of dried dreams hanging

                    like young boys & girls
                    playing totties on the streets
                    chasing each other giggling

this song from a distance says

                    our notes have deep roots
                    there is hope still
                    over the gloom   beyond the gloom

for those who forget
the smell of teargas
the rage of the sea

Time and words

to mxolisi nyezwa

each moment I read
      from pages of your book
            still I'm haunted
            by a pulsing voice
that makes all pains unnecessary

each moment
      someone quotes your words
      i am moved by the aura
      that they can still breathe
in this fresh poisonous atmosphere.

Before the night ends

let us smell the rain when it falls in this township
silence is heartbreaking it changes the direction of the
wind

i can hear my blood rushing through my veins
one day i will gather the clouds and give them to you

if it wasn't for literature, i would have been an empty skull
jazz spoke a thousand languages to me which will never
                                        be silenced

my child
when the universe burns in your hands
do not throw it to other men.

Qamata

your click sound overflows with love
appearing in the sky
surrounded by the stars, ancient as the sun
when i stand in my yard looking northward
i can feel your omnipresent spirit
i know you are there even when i'm drowning
in our capitalistic existence

Mankunku called the stars

Yakhal' inkomo
for what we lost
Mankunku called all the stars

He blew dust from the moon
so that light would be there above us
so that light would be there to smile at us

Yes we buried the pain –
but it still hurts us
into the first hours of the morning.

Horn screaming

to Zim Ngqawana

i feel your horn screaming
vadzimu
           vadzimu
where noise is silenced
screams trapped
with a note
from a bleeding heart
crowded with faces

           ingoma yakho
i feel it in the air
combining restless souls
in *zimphonic* suites
"mayenzeke intando yakho"
a voice moans like a futile wind
leaving a soul lying on dust
one among many

           zim-zim
this way i'm with you
the tears which hide
the gathering of clouds

           zimology
in cold silence
your spirit crowds me
your *san songs*
are the light coming through
to a sad-eyed blackman
today, i begin to live
a brief solace.

The trumpet note

Screams through a steel throat
Composes revolts on narrow streets
Declarations of anger
Burning and looting
Gasp of surviving
Without spitting at god

A note counts my wounds publicly
Telling me I'm bleeding
Someone is yelling at the back
"Kukude ebhofolo indawo yamageza"

I borrowed myself from the ground
I took my bags and i followed them
And my heart bleeds no more

With all the sounds of the universe
What are these that i have gathered
Which have left footprints in my chest

In the morning

today i understand
why some men
jump from the van stadens bridge
or hang themselves from the ceiling

silently i know
i could not stand emptiness
without you
i could not survive a day
without the hiss from the kettle
as you make coffee for me

our confrontations and arguments
i take them as flashes of lightning
and in the morning
the sky turns blue

since i married you
i have discovered
that tears can mean many things.

On this day

today
the morning sea was grey from a distance
splashing pieces of sadness
tearing dense clouds into tears

in the evening
i found myself without you

i won't let them take you away
from me.

Finding love

to my wife dieketso

i found love in a storm
in my country
in kwazakhele
in streets that smell of violence
where terror rules

i lifted my arms
to catch a shooting star
my eyes are satisfied

i find myself laughing at death
and holding someone
who comforts me
without any regrets.

I love you

after eight hours in a dense mist
of planting my flesh
in someone's garden

i want nothing except you
whatever they take
you renew it with a smile
your voice lasts longer
than their insults and orders

i love the happiness you induce
in me and my days
i love your forgiving eyes
that always look on the bright side
lifting your head
under the armpit of the wind
breathing on my neck.

Poem for you

Pain grows like a weed
In the world every day
And this township has taken
Too much from me,

I don't want the sky to weep for me
And spaza shops to close
I don't want the cries to drag on
I just want the silence to stay a little longer

I'll keep my word
In the next 24 hours
I'll write a poem for you
A poem with an aroma of impepho
Humming birds and water.

Written in silence

i do not have a title yet
it will only be four lines
i will read them on your funeral

> *under the rotten star*
> *only the sky is eternal*
> *and the black earth that feeds us*
> *rest now if god has not forgotten you*

i hope i won't break
and not grieve for too long

do the same for me
if i kiss the dust first.

Beginning of a song

To a violence of images
From our streets
A dead halt
Deafening absence of compassion
No visible dreams
But still i belong here

The old man with big glasses
Pushing a wheelbarrow
Collecting food for his piglets
Found a child in a black plastic bag
Curled, dead
He called the people
The sun went slowly blind

Women began to sing in tears
From the depths of the sea
Sending off a child to her ancestors
Calling and calling them
The moon opened a cloud like a window
To welcome the new spirit
I push the sunrise

Printed in the United States
By Bookmasters